Aberdeenshire Library and Information Service
www.aberdeenshire.gov.uk/libraries
Renewals Hotline 01224 661511

WELCH, Ian

Greatest
moments of boxing

D1076178

Greatest
MOMENTS OF
BOXING

This edition first published in the UK in 2007
By Green Umbrella Publishing

© Green Umbrella Publishing 2008

www.gupublishing.co.uk

Publishers: Jules Gammond and Vanessa Gardner

Printed and bound in China

ISBN: 978-1-906229-43-6

Greatest
MOMENTS OF
BOXING

by IAN WELCH

CONTENTS

CONTENTS

JOE LOUIS v MAX SCHMELING
1936

It was *the* fight of the decade, American Joe Louis against Germany's finest, Max Schmeling, in a battle of the Allies versus Hitler's Nazis. Professional boxing was among the few integrated sports in the United States at that time, and Louis was a hero to American Blacks while Hitler was apparently mortified that the German hero would be fighting a "negro".

Joseph Louis Barrow was born on 13 May 1914 in Alabama, into a poor family deep in the south of the United States. Moving to Detroit 10 years later, Louis was supposed to be learning the violin but instead went to boxing lessons. After winning the Golden Gloves award for light-heavyweights in 1934, he turned professional and won 12 fights within the next 12 months.

Two fights against former heavyweight champions followed in quick succession for the rising star – Primo Carnera and Max Baer in June and September 1935 respectively… Louis stopped them both within six rounds. Then he met German Max Schmeling.

Schmeling was born near Brandenburg on 28 September 1905 and claimed the world title after an illegal punch by Jack Sharkey in 1930. He lost the rematch to Sharkey two years later on a controversial points decision. He fought just five times after World War II and never got another title shot before retiring in 1948. Germany's last heavyweight champion, his final fight was a 10-round defeat by Reidel Vogt in Berlin, 24 years after his professional debut, giving him figures of 56 wins (39 knockouts), 10 losses and four draws.

Schmeling had studied films of Louis boxing and identified a weakness in his style. He noticed that the Brown Bomber dropped his left hand to his side after jabbing rather than protect his chin and realised that – if he could overcome his fear to get in close enough – he could take advantage of this lapse in concentration and land one of his big right hooks.

On 19 June 1936, after rain postponed the fight a day, the undefeated Louis took on Max Schmeling. The fight began very cautiously with both fighters probing but, with two minutes of the fourth round gone, Schmeling got the opportunity he was looking for and landed a huge right-hook. Louis, visibly shaken, was then hit by a barrage of punches that put him on the canvas.

JOE LOUIS v MAX SCHMELING

GREATEST MOMENTS OF BOXING

Observers have described Louis as a punching bag following that incident, fighting on instinct and heart alone. Such was the battering that Louis was taking as the fight wore on that his mother Lillie had to be led away from the ring because she was so distressed. In the 12th round, Schmeling landed a couple of vicious punches that felled Louis yet again, but this time the Brown Bomber was unable to regain his feet.

German Minister of Propaganda Joseph Goebbels proclaimed Schmeling's victory as a triumph for both Germany and Hitlerism. The Nazi weekly journal *Das Schwarze Korps* (The Black Corps) commented: "Schmeling's victory was not only sport. It was a question of prestige for our race."

Louis went on to claim the heavyweight title the following year, knocking out James J Braddock in eight rounds to become the first black boxer since Jack Johnson to hold the title. He successfully defended his title against three challengers, including Tommy Farr who took the Brown Bomber to a points decision on 31 August 1937 after a gruelling 15-round contest. But the fight he was really looking forward to was the rematch with Schmeling in 1938. Indeed, he had insisted that he could not be called a champion until he had avenged his earlier defeat.

When the German arrived in New York, protesters demonstrated outside his hotel and chants of "Nazi! Nazi!" filled the air. Such was the political climate that newspapers suggested that Schmeling had claimed that a black man could not defeat him and that his winnings would go towards building more tanks for the German Army.

As it turned out, the hype surrounding the rematch on 22 June 1938 lasted longer than the contest itself. Schmeling (32) had weighed in just under five pounds lighter than the 24-year-old Louis and was on the ropes from the bell. Louis landed punch after punch before the German's knees caved in. After a short count, the fight was allowed to continue before the contender was on the canvas. Regaining his feet, Schmeling threw a total of two punches in the fight before his corner threw the towel in after just two minutes and four seconds of the contest.

Schmeling – who served as a German paratrooper in the Second World War – declared his opposition to the Nazis and received an award from the International Raoul Wallenberg Foundation for risking his life to hide two Jewish brothers during November 1938. He went on to develop a personal friendship with Louis and the two became such good friends that Schmeling paid for the American boxer's funeral arrangements when he died in 1981. Schmeling himself died in February 2005 at the age of 99.

ROCKY MARCIANO v JERSEY JOE WALCOTT
1952

Mention the name Rocky to anyone these days and most people will immediately think of the character in the Sylvester Stallone films *Rocky-Rocky Balboa* but the original was Rocky Marciano. He is the only heavyweight to go throughout his career undefeated, winning 49 fights and knocking out 43 opponents.

Marciano was born Rocco Francis Marchegiano on 1 September 1920 in Massachusetts to Italian immigrant parents. Five siblings followed and at school Marciano became a highly-rated sportsman with baseball as one of his specialist sports. But, after failing to make the big time with the bat, boxing captivated his attention and it was as a boxer that he found fame and fortune.

He learned his trade while serving in the US Army at the end of World War II but failed to impress promoter Al Weill in New York. Continuing as an amateur, Marciano earned his living as a factory worker before turning professional in 1947. He won his next 35 fights in a remarkable 146 rounds and moved up the ladder to challenge Rex Layne four years later. Winning in half a dozen rounds, Weill had a change of heart and agreed to manage Marciano. He lined up a fight with former world champion Joe Louis which Rocky won in the eighth round to give him a shot at the title held by "Jersey" Joe Walcott.

Walcott, born Arnold Raymond Cream in New Jersey on 31 January 1914 (his nickname came from comparisons to former world heavyweight champion Joe Walcott), had recently become the oldest man to win the heavyweight world title against Ezzard Charles. He had started boxing at the age of 16 and this was his fifth attempt at winning the belt. Two of his title challenges had been against the great Joe Louis, whom he had put on the canvas in each fight so it wasn't a foregone conclusion that the younger fighter would triumph.

Forty thousands fans were in Philadelphia's Munical Stadium – while another 140,000 watched the fight on the increasingly popular television set – and they were not disappointed. From the outset, Walcott threatened to knock the young pretender out and bludgeoned him

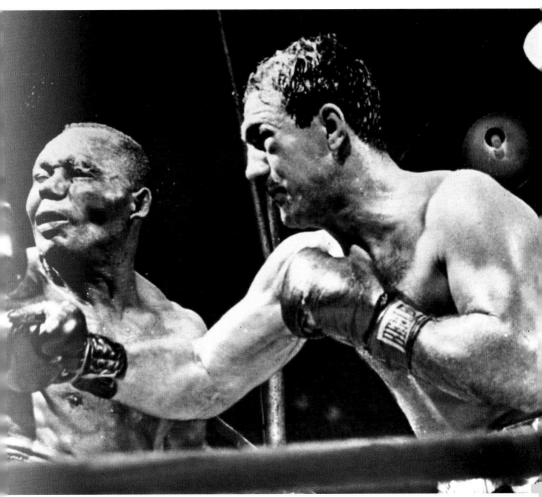

with his left and right hand in the opening round. The unexpected onslaught caught Marciano off guard and he was soon on the canvas, getting up at the count of four.

Walcott continued with this strategy but conceded defeat in round three and reverted to his normal style of boxing that included hit-and-run counter-attacks. The elder boxer looked the more accomplished of the two fighters as he waited patiently for an opening, holding his opponent when he deemed it was necessary, while Marciano relied on his ability to take whatever was thrown at him while attempting to land the knockout blow. And so the fight continued, but by the end of the 10th round Marciano was level on points so Walcott came out with all guns blazing. He claimed the next two rounds – with Marciano ending up heavily bruised and cut around the eyes – but was obviously tired as the bout entered its 13th episode.

With three rounds to go, it seemed that all Walcott had to do to retain his crown was to stay out of trouble so he threw a few jabs and withdrew onto the ropes. Marciano had other ideas, however, and launched a short overhand punch that landed on Walcott's head and the champion's knees began to wobble. Rocky threw a left-hander that grazed his opponent's head and then stepped back to watch Walcott cling to the middle rope before slumping to the canvas. The referee completed the count and then immediately turned the prone fighter over so that he could receive medical attention from doctors and his corner team.

This was the moment the challenger had been waiting for when he had promised to himself as a child in the Great Depression that he would find a way to make a better life…Rocky Marciano was the new heavyweight champion of the world.

Marciano defended his title with ease in a rematch with Walcott the following year with the fight ending in the first round after just 145 seconds. He successfully retained his title in a further five fights, although he was floored by Archie Moore in what turned out to be his final bout.

He decided to quit the ring in 1956 in order to spend more time with his family though some questioned whether he realised his own frailties and wanted to retire undefeated. Rocky Marciano died on 31 August 1969 at the age of 45 when the light plane he was a passenger in crashed short of an airfield in Iowa.

Jersey Joe Walcott became a popular figure around New York until his death on 25 February 1994.

CASSIUS CLAY v SONNY LISTON
1964

It was hardly the best preparation to the fight when Cassius Clay was sent sprawling by Henry Cooper in the fourth round of their 1963 bout. Luckily for the brash American, Cooper's tendency to cut easily flared up and the contest was stopped in the following round. Sonny Liston, however, had just come off the back of two first-round knockouts of world heavyweight champion Floyd Patterson.

Charles "Sonny" Liston was born in Arkansas on 8 May 1932, (although some sources claim he was born as early as 1927 but there is no proof of this), one of 17 children, and he experienced a harsh childhood with beatings a regular occurrence. As soon as he was a teenager, he ran away from his father and went to live with his mother but got involved with the Mafia as a bonebreaker. But he was soon serving a prison sentence for his part in an armed robbery of a petrol station (later in his career, this conviction would lead to calls for him to be barred from boxing) and it was while incarcerated that a priest noticed his pugilistic talent. His professional career kicked off in September 1953 with a first-round knockout of Don Smith and by the time he took on Clay his record stood at 35-1 with 25 knockouts.

Cassius Clay, on the other hand, was born in Kentucky on 17 January 1942 and won the Light Heavyweight gold medal at the 1960 Olympic Games in Rome. Having an unorthodox boxing style that relied on his ability to evade his opponent's hands rather than keeping his guard up, Clay defeated Tunney Hunsaker in six rounds to notch up his first professional victory in October 1960. Clay entered the ring on 25 February 1964 with a 19-0 record (including 15 knockouts).

At the weigh-in the previous day, Ali had been fined $1,500 for his behaviour that included his soon to be familiar taunt that he would "float like a butterfly and sting like a bee". The two fighters were reasonably similar in stature, with Clay being just over two inches taller than his opponent but with Liston enjoying a 4" reach advantage (Ali was also around 7lbs heavier).

The fight began with Clay showing his nimble footwork and speed around the ring which made it nearly impossible for Liston to hit his target. He persevered and did manage to connect with

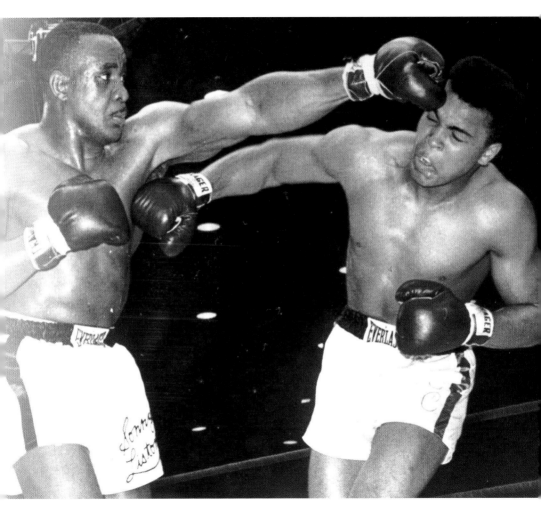

some punches but it was the agile Clay who made the early running with his precise jabs and combinations, although the champion did manage to pin the challenger to the ropes in round two. By the third round, however, Liston's face was beginning to show signs of trauma, with a cut under his left eye and a mouse under his right one.

Clay had a relatively quiet fourth round but complained to his corner at the bell that something was burning his eyes. It has never been proved what was affecting him although it has been speculated it was something Liston's cuts were being treated with. It has also been alleged that this was not the first time that one of Liston's opponents had suffered in this way.

Whatever the reason, Clay was advised by his corner to stay away from his opponent during the fifth round to give his eyes a chance to clear but he resumed hostilities in the sixth round with a vengeance. He landed several telling combinations and Sonny Liston remained on his stool as the bell rang for round seven complaining of a shoulder injury. The ever-modest Clay immediately jumped up onto the ropes and shouted "I'm the greatest!" – a nickname that quickly stuck (along with "Louisville Lip").

The two fighters met in a rematch that should have been held in November 1964 but which had to be postponed for six months as Clay – who had by now changed his name to Muhammad Ali – had to undergo surgery for a strangulated hernia. When it did take place, the fight proved to be controversial with Sonny Liston hitting the canvas in the first round following a soft Ali punch. Critics argue that it could not possibly have been a knockdown but referee Jersey Joe Walcott tried to contain Ali in a neutral corner rather than beginning the count. As Liston had been down for around 20 seconds when this was pointed out, Walcott awarded the fight to Ali.

Muhammad Ali went on to have one of the most successful careers in the history of boxing while Sonny Liston won 15 out of his 16 fights before his unexplained death in December 1970. He was found dead in his Las Vegas home but there was no apparent cause of death. It was suggested that he died from a heroin overdose but many have discounted this due to his phobia of needles.

MUHAMMAD ALI v GEORGE FOREMAN
1974

"Rumble in the Jungle" was now-notorious promoter Don King's first event and he had persuaded both world champion George Foreman and former champion Muhammad Ali to separately sign contracts with him promising them a $5 million purse. As he didn't have that kind of money, he searched for a sponsor whom he readily found in Zaire's President Mobutu Sésé.

George Foreman was born in Texas on 10 January 1949 and, despite being in trouble with the authorities during his youth, qualified for the United States Olympic team by the age of 19. He went on to win the Heavyweight gold medal at the 1968 Olympic Games in Mexico City and turned professional the following year. His first fight at this level was a three-round demolition of Don Waldheim at New York's Madison Square Garden in June of that year and he went on to fight another dozen times before Christmas, with only two going the distance.

He got his title shot against the undefeated "Smokin'" Joe Frazier who had claimed the belt from Jimmy Ellis in February 1970 and successfully defended his crown on four occasions (including against Muhammad Ali in 1971). "Big George" at 6' 3½", floored the champion six times in just two rounds to stun the boxing world. Foreman himself retained his crown after beating Jose Roman and Ken Norton before facing Ali on 30 October 1974.

Ali had defended his title eight times since his rematch with Sonny Liston but he had been forced to fight abroad for the majority of these bouts because of his altercation with the US authorities. In 1964, Ali failed the qualifying tests for the Armed Forces but when these were revised two years later he became eligible to be drafted to Vietnam. He refused to go, stating he was a conscientious objector but was stripped of his title by the boxing commission in 1967 and sentenced to five years' imprisonment. He fought both counts and was eventually readmitted to the boxing fraternity in 1970 with the Supreme Court reversing his conviction the following year. Ali did, however, officially retire on 1 February 1970 to allow the winner of the upcoming Joe Frazier v Jimmy Ellis unification bout to be considered the undisputed champion.

Foreman and Ali spent much of the summer training in Zaire (now the Democratic Republic of Congo) to acclimatise themselves with the fight originally scheduled for September. A cut above Foreman's eye, however, delayed the bout by a month.

The contest started with the more agile Ali easily outmanoeuvring the bigger man as planned but the Louisville Lip soon found that he was tiring by moving quickly around the ring and that his punches – he landed nine heavy right-hand leads in the first round alone – were hardly having any effect on Foreman. As a result, he changed his tactics and decided to let Foreman expend his energy throwing punches at him that he could dodge or absorb as the moment saw fit. He labelled this strategy "rope-a-dope" and it soon became obvious that it was working.

Foreman – who had won 37 of his previous 40 fights by knockout with his last eight being finished by the second round – was looking visibly tired as the fight went on and his face was starting to show signs of the well-timed counter punches that Ali was able to land. The challenger would also dupe his opponent into supporting his weight when they were in clinches, thereby forcing the champion to use up more precious energy in the stifling heat. He also taunted Foreman by telling him that his punches weren't hard enough.

As the fight drew on, the champion was rocked by Ali combinations in the fourth and fifth rounds but it was the left hook followed by a dynamite right in the eighth round that put an end to George Foreman's grip on the title. Foreman hit the deck but was slow regaining his feet and later suggested that he had been waiting for a signal from his corner that had come too late. In a huge upset, Ali had become only the second man – after Floyd Patterson – to regain the world heavyweight crown.

Many claim that this fight shows Ali – who went on to hold the title until losing to Leon Spinks in February 1978 – at perhaps his best, clearly demonstrating his ability to take a punch but it also implies that taking a pounding such as this has possibly contributed to the debilitating Parkinson's disease that afflicts Muhammad Ali today. Foreman – who did not fight again until January 1976 – and Ali have since become firm friends and it was Big George who helped his former rival up to the stage when the documentary film of this fight, *When We Were Kings*, won the 1996 Academy Award for Documentary Feature.

JOHN CONTEH v JORGE AHUMADA 1974

Wednesday 1 October 1974 saw John Conteh become the first Briton to hold the WBC Light Heavyweight title since Freddie Mills in 1950. The Liverpool-born boxer received the chance to contest this title when the American holder Bob Foster announced his retirement in September 1974.

Conteh, born on 27 May 1951, came from a large family – he had nine brothers and sisters – and first came to national prominence when he won Middleweight gold medal at the 1970 Commonwealth Games in Edinburgh with a victory over Titus Simba. Conteh's first professional fight was a first-round knockout of Okacha Boubekeur in October 1971. He then went on to beat Rudiger Schmidtke three years later to claim the European Light Heavyweight title and added the British and Commonwealth titles with a points decision over Chris Finnegan.

Jorge Ahumada, on the other hand, had already had a shot at the title and failed. The Argentinian (born on 6 January 1946) fought Bob Foster in June 1974 and emerged with a draw (143-148, 145-142, 144-144) after a 15-round battle. Ahumada had begun his professional career in January 1968 with a knockout of Eudoro Robledo in the fourth round and he came into this fight boasting 41 victories (22 knockouts), five losses and two draws.

Conteh came in on the back of 25 wins (with 19 knockouts) and just one defeat – a points decision against Eddie Duncan in October 1972 – and weighed just a quarter of a pound more than his opponent. Wembley Empire Pool in northwest London was the venue for the fight and the sell-out crowd were anticipating a home victory.

Conteh came out fast in his usual determined style and, although the first three rounds were a closely contested affair, began to take control of the fight. He had obviously managed to remain calm in the hours running up to the fight, despite all the media hype, as he utilised all his combative skills. Conteh then began to find his way through Ahumada's defences and started landing accurate left hooks and overhand rights which did his scorecard no harm at all.

The middle section of the fight saw both men stand toe-to-toe, each trying to outpunch the other. Ahumada, who with five defeats already to his name was used to being punched, took it all in his stride and Conteh's tactics seemed to be having no effect on the Argentinian. But for the last three rounds, Conteh put in a concerted effort and his brutal barrage left its tell-tale signs on Ahumada's face as he finished the fight with his left eye closed.

Referee Harry Gibbs – the only scorer of the fight – immediately raised Conteh's hand and the nation hailed a new world champion. Gibbs had given Conteh the victory with a score of 147-142 and there was mention after the fight of trying to talk Foster out of retirement. As it turned out, Foster declined the offer but his "retirement" lasted less than a year anyway.

When his hand had been held up by the referee, Conteh joked "I thought he was my fairy godmother!" While the boxer's mother, never one to resort to corporal punishment, had declared before the fight that she'd "slug him one if he lost."

Conteh had had to relinquish his hold on his European, Commonwealth and British titles in order to take this fight, but he only won the WBC version of the belt because the WBA would not recognise the bout. Victor Galindez took on Len Hutchins for the vacant WBA Light Heavyweight title in December 1974 and gave a shot to Ahumada in June 1975. This was the Argentine's third and last chance of claiming a world title and he lost by a unanimous decision after 15 rounds. He fought twice more that year before heading into retirement.

Conteh, on the other hand, defended his title successfully three times over the next three years. In March 1975, he took on Lonnie Bennett but the fight was stopped in the fifth round as the American suffered a badly cut eye. In October the following year, his opponent was Mexican Yaqui Lopez and Conteh won a split decision after the 15-round fight in Copenhagen before facing Len Hutchins in Liverpool the following March. He stopped the American in the third round but his title was stripped from him by the boxing authorities who did not rate the calibre of his opponents.

Conteh had three chances to regain his WBC Light Heavyweight crown but failed. He was the victim of an outrageous points decision against Mate Parlov in June 1978 and had two fights against Matthew Saad Muhammad in the space of five months in Atlantic City. He lost the first fight when the American won a unanimous decision (142-146, 143-144, 141-146) and the second bout ended in the fourth round but Conteh looked a pale comparison of his title-winning days.

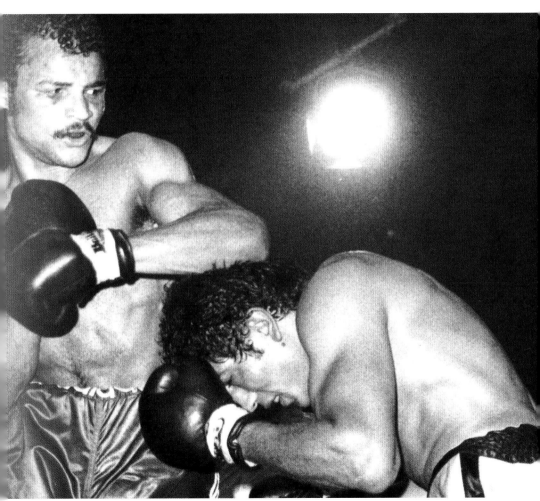

SUGAR RAY LEONARD v WILFRED BENITEZ
1979

After the retirement of the legendary Muhammad Ali on 6 September 1979, "Sugar" Ray Leonard had taken over the mantle of the most popular boxer in the world. On 30 November that year he lined up in Las Vegas's Caesar's Palace against Wilfred Benitez to contest his first world title and provided a dramatic finale to a classic boxing bout.

Leonard – born on 17 May 1956 in North Carolina and named after the legendary blues singer Ray Charles – started boxing at the age of 14. By the time he was 20, he had won a Light Welterweight gold medal at the 1976 Olympics, triumphing over Cuban Andrés Aldama in Montreal.

He turned professional and won his first bout in February 1977 by a unanimous decision after six rounds (30-24, 30-24, 30-24 against Luis Vega). By the time he fought his first world title contest in 1979, he had won all 25 of his fights, 14 of them by knockout. It is alleged that Leonard earned an amazing $3 million from these fights which, together with his $1 million purse for facing Benitez, was not a bad return for less than three years as a professional. (It is also claimed that Leonard eventually earned a massive $45 million from his escapades in the ring!)

Wilfred Benitez (born in New York on 12 September 1958) was a child prodigy whose talents were recognised early on by his father who came from one of Puerto Rico's most notorious boxing families (brothers Frankie and Gregorio both tried their hand at boxing in the 1970s but neither managed to get a shot at a world title). Nicknamed "El Radar", Wilfred learnt his trade in a New York gym and became a professional in 1973. It would be unheard of these days for a 15-year-old to be allowed to box professionally, but he was good enough to be ranked by both the WBA and WBC.

His first fight was against Hiram Santiago and ended in a first-round knockout in November 1973 and he had racked up 25 straight victories (20 knockouts) by the time he fought his first world title bout in March 1976. He beat WBA Light Welterweight holder Antonio Cervantes by

SUGAR RAY LEONARD v WILFRED BENITEZ

a split decision (148-144, 147-142, 145-147) to become the youngest ever world champion at the age of 17. He later claimed the WBC Welterweight title with a split decision victory (148-143, 146-143, 142-146) over Carlos Palomino in January 1979.

With both fighters undefeated (Benitez came into the fight having won 38 and drawn one of his 39 fights) going into this clash, the audience knew they were in for an entertaining night but few could have predicted that it would end in such a dramatic fashion.

The fight started off with both boxers cautiously waiting for the other to launch an attack while they defended and counter-punched. The first two rounds proved a rather dull affair before Leonard caught Benitez with a left hook in the third round that sent him to the canvas. The champion quickly regained his feet and the pace of the contest picked up.

The pair began trading punches, with Benitez punching over the top to land on his opponent's head with his right, while Leonard was utilizing his left hook under El Radar's high right hand. But in the sixth round, a clash of heads left Leonard with a bump and Benitez with a cut…fortunately, these injuries didn't trouble either fighter and normal service resumed.

Leonard and Benitez fought a toe-to-toe battle in the ninth round that saw Sugar Ray come out on top and the Puerto Rican took such a battering in the 11th that it looked as if a knockout was just around the corner. Leonard connected with a vicious left hook that drove the champion into the ropes then followed that up with a fierce right that knocked Benitez's gumshield out of his mouth. He recovered and fought his way back into the contest although the majority of the accurate and destructive punches were launched by Leonard in the 12th round.

As Benitez rose to his feet at the bell signifying the final round, the challenger allegedly said "Oh my God, he's still standing!" before renewing the onslaught. It looked as if the fight would have to be decided by the judges but Leonard found the knockout punch just seconds before the final bell. Although Benitez got back to his feet, referee Carlos Padilla called a stop to the fight with just six seconds left on the clock.

Benitez went on to win the WBC Light Middleweight title with a victory over Maurice Hope in May 1981 and successfully defended it against Carlos Santos and Roberto Duran before losing to Thomas Hearns (see page 34 for details of Leonard's own battles with Duran) before eventually retiring in 1990. Leonard went on to win world titles at Light Middleweight, Middleweight, Super Middleweight and Light Heavyweight in a career that spanned 20 years.

MUHAMMAD ALI v
LARRY HOLMES
1980

Thursday 2 October 1980, didn't just see the end of a legend, it saw the destruction of the Greatest. This was supposed to be Muhammad Ali's opportunity to rewrite the record books and become the only boxer ever to win four world heavyweight titles but it ended with many calling the fight a sham.

Ali – born on 17 January 1942 in Kentucky – had already become the only man to win three titles when he reclaimed the WBA Heavyweight title from Leon Spinks with a unanimous decision (10-4, 10-4, 11-4) in September 1978. Spinks had inflicted only Ali's third defeat in 58 fights when he had torn the WBC and WBA belts from his grip the previous April in a split decision (140-145, 141-144, 143-142). The rematch would have been to contest both belts, but the WBC stripped theirs from Spinks when he chose to defend it against Ali instead of their number one contender Ken Norton.

So Ali returned to training after challenging his former sparring partner to a title fight. The contest took place more than two years after Ali had last been in the ring and disturbing stories came out of his camp after the fight. It was claimed that the results of Ali's medical exam had been hushed up and that in fact it had revealed tingling in his hands, slurred speech and a hole in the membrane of his brain.

Larry Holmes, born on 3 November 1949 in Georgia, turned professional in 1973 and won his first world title by beating Ken Norton in a closely-fought encounter in June 1978 that ended in a split decision (143-142, 143-142, 142-143). "The Easton Assassin" went on to win his next 20 fights before a unanimous decision (142-145, 142-143, 142-145) saw him lose to Michael Spinks in September 1985 in his 49th fight. If he had won against Spinks, he would have equalled the great Joe Louis' record of 49 consecutive victories.

At the initial bell, Holmes immediately launched an attack on Ali with a left hook, a body shot and another hook that stunned the challenger. The champion convincingly won the first round despite Ali's attempt at a knockout punch when he jabbed and then followed this up

MUHAMMAD ALI v LARRY HOLMES   31

with a right cross. It connected with Holmes's chin, but did not have the effect that Ali was hoping for. The second round continued with more of the same: Ali was talking a good fight in his attempts to goad Holmes into making a mistake but his punches weren't getting through. The champion's were, however, and by the end of the round Ali's left cheek was marked.

The fourth round saw Holmes set Ali's nose bleeding while the challenger again looked for the miracle punch. Holmes, meanwhile, continued jabbing away at Ali and this was starting to take its toll on the former champion. Ali tried his rope-a-dope tactics that had worked so well on George Foreman in 1974 (see page 18) but Holmes was aware of this strategy and merely timed his punches to perfection without overly exerting himself.

The fifth round saw Ali come into the centre of the ring seemingly more agile and nimble-footed than he had been so far but a couple of punches from Holmes soon returned him to his normal speed. Ali was basically being used as a sparring partner, there to hit with no real danger of Holmes being hit himself. Ali tried to get his jab going in the sixth round to no avail. While Holmes's punches all seemed to be hitting the mark, Ali could not find a way through the champion's defences and boos were soon ringing round Caesar's Palace in Las Vegas.

The fight carried on like this until the ninth round, with Holmes neatly picking off his opponent with a variety of punches while Ali was unable to do anything about it except absorb the blows. One of those punches landed in the area of his kidneys and after the bell trainer Angelo Dundee asked Ali if he really wanted to carry on but the self-proclaimed Greatest was persuaded to continue by another of his cornermen. In the end, Dundee made the decision after another whitewash in the 10th round and Ali failed to come out for the bell at the start of the 11th.

Statistics were later published that showed that only 10 of Ali's punches in the 10 rounds had actually found their target and it was later claimed by Ali that the side effects of a drug he was taking to cure a thyroid condition caused his below-par performance.

Holmes would later admit that he hadn't boxed to the best of his ability out of respect – and possibly pure sympathy – for Ali, who would attempt one more comeback. He fought the up-and-coming Trevor Berbick in December 1981 but lost to the man 12 years his junior by a unanimous decision (94-97, 94-99, 94-99).

SUGAR RAY LEONARD v ROBERTO DURAN
1980

Two of the greatest fighters the world has ever seen clashed twice during the year of 1980. "Sugar" Ray Leonard and Roberto Duran entertained the boxing audiences with two spectacular clashes for the WBC Welterweight title in June 1980 at Montreal's Olympic Stadium and then five months later at the Superdome in New Orleans.

Sugar Ray Leonard – born on 17 May 1956 in North Carolina – first won his title against Wilfred Benitez (see page 26) in November 1979 before defending it in a fourth-round knockout of Dave "Boy" Green four months later.

Robert Duran was born on 16 June 1951 in Panama and won his first professional fight in February 1968 with a unanimous decision over Carlos Mendoza. He had previously won both the WBA and WBC Lightweight belts and came into this fight with just one loss in 73 bouts.

In the first encounter, the Panamanian started strongly and soon landed an overhand right in the second round that began the damage. He followed this up with a left hook to Leonard's body and then a right that sent the champion into the ropes. The next two rounds saw Duran continue to dominate, scoring massive punches with his left hooks and overhand rights.

Leonard was allowing Duran to box in close quarters, something his corner had wanted to avoid, but the champion did come back into the contest in the fifth round when he started to find his range with his left hook. He, like his opponent, concentrated on body shots aimed at weakening the other boxer but it was Duran who was enjoyed the majority of the scoring.

Leonard's corner implored him to stop trying to guess what his opponent would do and get his punches in first and in the later rounds he did try this strategy. The 13th proved to be the most exciting of the night, with Duran targeting Leonard's body with a fierce right to the body that forced the champion to drop his arms to fend off the next blow. Unfortunately for him, the next blow was a left hook to his head. The champion recovered to land a left hook of his own among other punches which saw Duran on the ropes this time.

GREATEST MOMENTS OF BOXING

Both fighters appeared tired in the final two rounds and each would have been glad to hear the final bell. Duran was the happier of the two when the referee announced the judges' unanimous verdict: 144-145, 147-148, 144-146.

While Leonard could at least console himself with the biggest payday in sporting history at $10 million, the boxer with the normally silky skills had lost his title to the brawler from Panama and he wanted revenge. He would only have to wait five months for his chance.

The rematch turned into something of a farce when Duran pulled up with two minutes and 44 seconds of the eighth round gone and conceded the fight. He later attributed his decision to the stomach cramps that he claimed he had been suffering since round five but then went on to state "I've gotten tired of the sport. I feel it's time for me to retire."

The spectacular had commenced with Ray Charles – after whom Leonard was named – singing "America The Beautiful" but then the hostilities began in earnest. Leonard controlled the first two rounds with consummate ease, landing telling left hooks, right hands and beautifully timed combinations that shook Duran. The champion tried to utilise the same tactics that had won him the first fight and for a while in the third round it looked like it was working but Leonard was wise to this strategy and quickly moved away from the ropes to give himself space to work.

Although he showed no outward signs of any discomfort, Duran was beginning to suffer from alleged stomach cramps in round five but by the end of the sixth round he is supposed to have told his interpreter that his arms were getting weak. Leonard was in total control of the seventh round, landing punch after punch and even beginning to taunt his opponent. And then it was all over, Duran saying to the referee "No más, no más!" (the Spanish for "no more").

An hour after the fight, the Louisiana State Athletic Commission announced it was withholding the Panamanian's share of the money pending an examination but a week later a flu-ridden Duran appeared live on television to withdraw his decision to retire.

He later won Light Middleweight and Middleweight world titles and fought Leonard for the WBC Super Middleweight belt in 1989 (losing a unanimous decision) before finally retiring in 2001 at the age of 50. Leonard himself went on to win Light Middleweight, Middleweight, Super Middleweight and Light Heavyweight titles before retiring in 1997.

BARRY McGUIGAN v EUSEBIO PEDROZA
1985

Barry McGuigan was one of the most popular boxers of the 1980s, not just with his fellow Irishmen but across the whole of the UK. His victory against Eusebio Pedroza in front of a capacity crowd at Queen's Park Rangers' Loftus Road stadium ended the Panamanian's seven-year reign as WBA Featherweight champion.

Barry "The Clones Cyclone" McGuigan was born on 28 February 1961 in Clones, Co Monaghan in the Republic of Ireland. His father, Pat McGuigan, represented his country at the Eurovision Song Contest and was a great inspiration to his son. Indeed, McGuigan has been quoted as saying that his father's death was one of the reasons he retired when he did.

McGuigan made his professional debut in May 1981 with a second-round knockout of Selvin Bell and won the British Featherweight title two years later with a victory over Vernon Penprase. The European belt followed seven months after that courtesy of knocking out Valerio Nati in the sixth round in Belfast's King's Hall.

Eusebio "El Alacrán" Pedroza was born on 2 March 1953 in Panama City and turned professional with a fourth-round knockout of Julio Garcia in December 1973. His first shot at a world title came in April 1976 when he took on Alfonso Zamora for the WBA Bantamweight crown but was knocked down twice in the second round. He had to wait a further four years for another chance, this time against WBA Featherweight champion Cecilio Lastra. Pedroza scored a technical knockout victory over the Spaniard and went on to be a worthy champion.

McGuigan's preparations had taken a downturn when he pulled a ligament in his left arm on the Monday before the fight. Indeed, he explained afterwards that it had hampered his left jab during the fight…not that his fans needed any consolation. McGuigan came into the fight with a record of 26 victories (with 23 by knockout) and one loss. That defeat had occurred in only his third fight, a points decision against Peter Eubank in August 1981. Pedroza, on the other hand, boasted 38 victories (25 knockouts), three losses and one draw. McGuigan was 2" shorter than his opponent but there was only a quarter of a pound difference in their weight.

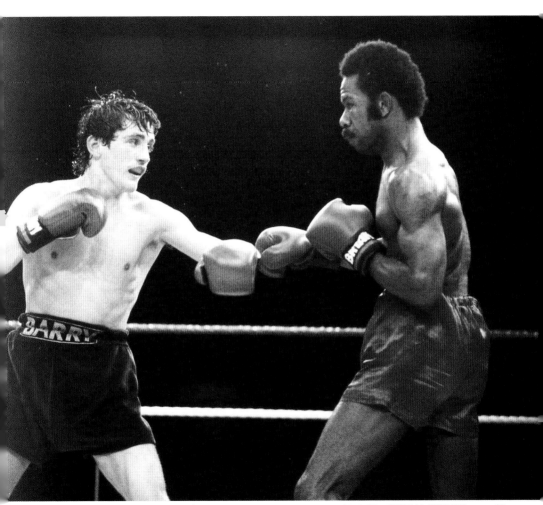

BARRY McGUIGAN v EUSEBIO PEDROZA

GREATEST MOMENTS OF BOXING

The pace was frantic from the outset with McGuigan and Pedroza both trading punches in a flurry of activity. It was an exhausting contest and both boxers were returning to their corners after each round in need of a well-earned rest. The turning point came in the seventh round when McGuigan caught the champion with a left and right combination that stunned Pedroza. The Panamanian crashed into the ropes and hit the canvas but recovered to beat the count.

The ninth round saw the Clones Cyclone rock Pedroza again after another combination and El Alacrán was obviously getting worried because referee Stanley Christodoulou had to warn him about low punches. Although McGuigan appeared to tire towards the end of the fight, he carried on pounding away at his opponent. The tactics worked because when the referee came to announce the judges' verdict he held McGuigan's arm aloft. The judges had given him a unanimous decision (148-138, 147-140, 149-139) and the title of world champion.

McGuigan had been hoping to fight in Belfast but this proved unfeasible, and the streets that had been deserted during the fight filled with people celebrating the moment the decision was announced. On their return to the city, he and his wife were paraded through the streets in a massive public display of affection.

McGuigan's victory not only brought Pedroza's seven-year hold on the belt to an end, it also prevented him from going on to equal the record for the most successful defences of the Featherweight title. Abe Attell had won 21 consecutive fights from 1906-10 while Pedroza was aiming for number 20 that night.

Pedroza lost a split decision against Edgar Castro the following year and then announced his retirement. He was tempted back into the ring five years later and emerged victorious from his clash with Tomas Rodriguez. He won two more fights – against Jorge Romero and Tomas Quinones – before losing to Mauro Gutierrez and hanging up his gloves for good.

McGuigan defended his title – against Bernard Taylor and Danilo Cabrera – before succumbing to the young Steve Cruz in Las Vegas in June 1986. Unaccustomed to the heat, McGuigan (who had been ahead on points half way through the bout) suffered dehydration and exhaustion as he lost the fight on a close points decision (142-143, 139-143, 141-142). He temporarily retired before attempting a year-long comeback that ended with a defeat at the hands of Jim McDonnell. His eye was badly cut and the referee stopped the fight in the fourth round. McGuigan has since gone on to become a successful TV commentator.

MIKE TYSON v
TREVOR BERBICK
1986

While the boxing community were well acquainted with "Iron" Mike Tyson before his 22 November 1986 fight with WBC Heavyweight titleholder Trevor Berbick, the whole world knew his name and were aware of his potential after the contest had finished. Tyson stopped the reigning champion in the second round of their clash at Las Vegas's Hilton Hotel to become the youngest ever Heavyweight champion in the history of the sport at the age of 20 years, four months and 22 days.

Michael Tyson was born in New York on 30 June 1966 but lost his father when he was just two years old. He was a victim of bullying by older children because of his high-pitched voice and lisp so learned to retaliate. He was constantly in trouble with the authorities and ended up in a juvenile detention centre where his boxing talent was noticed by one of the guards. He introduced him to legendary trainer Cus D'Amato who took the young Tyson under his wing and honed his craft.

Tyson's first professional fight was against Hector Mercedes in March 1985 and it ended in a first-round knockout victory for the debutant. He fought almost every month – sometimes with more than one bout per month – and within the next 18 months he had racked up 27 victories, 25 of those by knockout. Only James Tillis and Mitch Green managed to go the distance with the boxer who was being labelled "the baddest man on the planet". Tyson (5' 10") was later named by *Ring* magazine as the 14th greatest fighter of all time in 1999.

James Berbick was born on 1 August 1955 in Jamaica and represented his country at the 1976 Montreal Olympic Games. He turned professional the same year and came into this fight with a record of 32 victories (23 knockouts), four defeats and one draw. Apart from winning a world title – against Pinklon Thomas in March 1986 – Berbick's other claim to fame is that he was the last man to fight the legendary Muhammad Ali. In December 1981, he took on the Greatest and won a unanimous decision after 10 rounds.

The challenger – who was renowned for the power of his punching – had come at Berbick from the bell. Berbick's mistake, however, was to stand toe-to-toe and try to trade punches with the

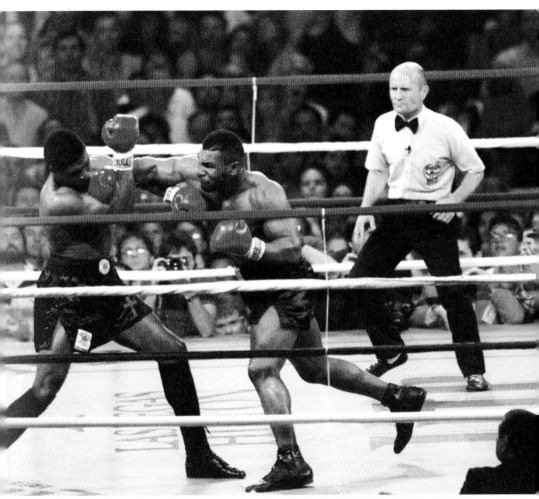

youngster from Brooklyn. Tyson repeatedly caught him with his ferocious left hook and his big right hand and Berbick was almost battered into submission in the first round while he looked for a telling uppercut. No matter how hard Berbick tried to keep his guard up to prevent Tyson from landing his punches, Iron Mike's left hook managed to find a way around the bigger man's defences. With seconds left in the first round, Tyson caught Berbick with a left hook and followed it up with a smashing right to send the champion staggering across the ring. With the Canadian just trying to make it through to the bell, Tyson could sense victory but was unable to deliver the knockout blow.

Tyson came out at the bell eager to continue what he had started and caught Berbick with several big punches in the opening seconds to send him to the canvas. While Tyson remained patient and kept throwing big right hands, Berbick hadn't fully recovered and seemed more intent on trying to hang on to Tyson to prevent him throwing any more punches. A right to Berbick's body was followed by an uppercut to his head and the champion was on the deck for the second time. Only this time he failed to recover; as he tried to regain his feet, he fell over again and staggered around the ring until referee Mills Lane called a halt to the contest. He later explained his decision by saying: "…to allow somebody to get hit in that condition, that's criminal."

"I was trying hard to prove to myself that I could take his best shot," the dethroned champion explained, the blemished area around his right eye showing the legacy of Tyson's punching. "He punches pretty hard."

Although Tyson claimed after the fight that, as well as being the youngest ever champion, he also planned on being the oldest, his career took a few odd twists and turns as he fell foul of the law. A rape conviction in 1992 saw him serve three years of his six-year sentence although he was never the same fighter after that incident and seemed to be constantly in the headlines for the wrong reasons.

Berbick continued boxing until 2000 but never regained his world title. He was found dead at a church in Norwich, Jamaica six years later with multiple head wounds. The weapon had been a 2" thick steel pipe and he died at the scene from his injuries aged 51. His 20-year-old nephew and his 18-year-old friend were charged with his murder.

SUGAR RAY LEONARD v MARVIN HAGLER 1987

Having been out of the ring for almost three years, not many gave "Sugar" Ray Leonard much of a chance when he met "Marvellous" Marvin Hagler to contest the WBC Middleweight crown in Caesar's Palace in Las Vegas on 6 April 1987. Hagler might well have put his WBA belt on the line as well but the World Boxing Association stripped him of their title when he arranged to fight the unranked Leonard.

This wasn't the first time Leonard had taken a break from boxing; he spent more than two years between fights after beating Bruce Finch for the WBA and WBC Welterweight titles. Indeed, since triumphing over Thomas Hearns in September 1981, Leonard had only fought twice; against Finch in February 1982 (a third-round victory after which he required surgery for a detached retina) and Kevin Howard in May 1984 (who had knocked him down for the only time in his career before turning it round for a ninth-round win).

Leonard – born on 17 May 1956 in North Carolina – came into the fight at 5' 10" and 160lbs with a record of 33 wins (24 knockouts) and one defeat (against Roberto Duran in 1980). There was just one inch difference in the two boxers' height, with Hagler (born on 23 May 1954 in New Jersey) slightly shorter but weighing the same. His record on entering the ring was an impressive 62 victories (52 knockouts), two losses (both early in his career in 1976) and one draw.

The start of the fight proved to be a cagey affair with Hagler in the centre of the ring waiting for the challenger to come within range and Leonard dancing round the outside of the ring. This was all going to plan for Leonard, who did not want to get drawn into a brutal brawl with Hagler but would rather use his speed to outmanoeuvre his opponent while picking his punches.

This continued throughout the opening rounds as Leonard would weave in through Hagler's defences to land a telling punch before dodging the counter-attack or embracing his opponent in a clinch that kept his arms out of harm's way. While Leonard scored well with these tactics, Hagler's persistence meant that he was back in the fight as it approached midway.

The contest became more of a slogging match as the bout progressed with Leonard perfectly at ease in a standing fight with Hagler although he did wobble after being hit in the ninth round. As it turned out, Leonard's scoring increased when he was on the ropes and having to lash out to fend off the champion although it didn't appear that his punches were doing any damage. It was the final three rounds that seemed to clinch the title for Leonard, as he repeatedly landed more and more combinations that excited the crowd.

At the end, referee Richard Steele announced the judges' split decision (118-110, 113-115, 115-113), a verdict that did not lie easy with Hagler who claimed "I feel in my heart I'm still champion. I felt I beat him in the last three rounds." The fight was good for both boxers' purses, however, with Leonard earning a guaranteed $11 million and Hagler $12 million.

The manner of the defeat proved hard to stomach though and Hagler quit the ring when he was denied the opportunity of a rematch. Instead, he moved to Italy and he starred in such films as *Indio* (1989) and its sequel *Indio 2* (1991), *Across Red Nights* and *Cyberflic* (both 1997). He is also a regular commentator on fight night television.

Leonard went on to fight Donny Lalonde for the WBC Light Heavyweight and the vacant WBC Super Middleweight crowns in November 1988, winning in the ninth round. He then fought two of his archrivals in the space of six months. First up was a rematch with Thomas Hearns whom he had already beaten in September 1981. They contested the WBC and WBO Super Middleweight titles in June 1989 which resulted in an unsatisfactory draw (113-112, 112-112, 112-113).

Leonard then engaged Roberto Duran for the third time. They had previously met twice in 1980 (see page 34) with one victory apiece so this was the decider. The contest went the distance for the second time and Leonard registered a 2-1 score with a unanimous decision (119-109, 116-111, 120-110) over the veteran Panamanian.

In his next fight, in February 1991, Leonard was on the wrong end of a unanimous decision, losing (103-119, 104-120, 110-116) against Terry Norris in a contest for the WBC Light Middleweight title. The last time Sugar Ray Leonard graced the ring was an amazing six years later when he took on Hector Camacho for the IBC Middleweight crown in March 1997. The years had caught up with him and he retired after the fifth-round defeat at the age of 40 but continued his interest in boxing starring as co-host and mentor in the reality TV show *The Contender*.

JAMES "BUSTER" DOUGLAS v MIKE TYSON
1990

It was the day the underdog triumphed! The undefeated "Iron" Mike Tyson faced James "Buster" Douglas in his 10th defence of his WBC, WBA and IBF Heavyweight titles in a fight that the champion was expected to win with ease. Some had questioned the commitment and stamina shown by Douglas in previous fights and an early result was anticipated in Tokyo.

Mike Tyson – born on 30 June 1966 – had claimed the WBC crown from Trevor Berbick in 1986 (see page 42) and within 12 months added the WBA and IBF versions with unanimous decisions over James Smith and Tony Tucker respectively.

At 6' 3", James Douglas – born in Ohio on 7 April 1960 – enjoyed a 5" height and 12" reach advantage over Tyson. He had turned professional in 1981 and had a shot at the vacant IBF Heavyweight title in 1987. Tony Tucker stopped him in the 10th round for the fourth defeat of his career.

The first round began with both fighters biding their time, taking jabs when they could but Tyson was the more accurate of the two. After being warned for hitting on the break, Tyson was hit by a body and head shot but both boxers traded a couple of head blows just before the bell. Douglas got the better of the second round with a powerful three-shot combination and several head shots while the champion still seemed to be finding his feet. Tyson did finish the round strongly, though. The third saw more of the same, with Douglas landing effective jabs, rights and an uppercut while Tyson was struggling to make any effective contribution.

He did better towards the end of the next round, although his opponent's corner was complaining about the use of elbows. The champion landed several left hooks and body shots and the crowd at Japan's Tokyo Dome sensed they were about to witness a real brawl. The fifth round saw Tyson again attack the challenger but there was no continuity in his boxing. True, he landed some decent blows but they didn't have the knockout power that

people had come to expect from him and Douglas was able to soak it up and launch counter-attacks of his own.

The sixth round was the slowest of the fight and it ended with Tyson showing signs of damage above his left eye. There was a lot of clinching and, while Douglas did land a short uppercut, Tyson had the best of the encounter with a couple of lefts to the heads and a right to the body. The next round saw the champion being warned about low punches but he did manage to get in some useful shots. Tyson again landed more punches than his opponent including some fierce body and head shots.

The eighth round was more explosive. Douglas was looking jaded and threw fewer punches although he did register a solid jab and a couple of shots to his opponent's head in the opening seconds. Tyson responded with a left hand and a couple of short rights to the head but the middle section of this round saw very little happening. The challenger looked to be finishing strongly with a barrage of punches to the head and body before Tyson launched a right uppercut that sent Douglas to the deck. He regained his feet by the count of nine and was saved from any further punishment by the bell. Tyson returned to the battle arena with the intention of ending the contest there and then but Douglas caught him with a huge right. With his left eye almost shut, the champion landed a couple of lefts to his opponent's head but Douglas knocked him onto the ropes with a right that obviously hurt him. Three more punches followed before a wobbly Tyson managed to get hold of Douglas but the challenger managed to land another right to Tyson's head just before the bell.

Tyson opened the hostilities in the 10th round with a right hander but Douglas came back strongly with a two-shot combination, five jabs without response and an uppercut that hurt the champion even more. This was followed by a four-shot combination that knocked Tyson down, his gumshield falling out as he hit the deck. Tyson was still trying to get to his feet as referee Octavio Meyran counted him out.

Douglas went on to lose his titles to Evander Holyfield in his first defence as a result of a third-round knockout. He would get one more title shot, against Lou Savarese, for the vacant IBA Heavyweight title in June 1998 but was knocked down three times in the first round before retiring the following year. Tyson's next title fight saw a third-round stoppage of Frank Bruno in March 1996 for the WBC belt.

CHRIS EUBANK v NIGEL BENN
1990

The rivalry between Chris Eubank and Nigel Benn in the early 1990s equalled that of any two fighters either before or since. There were the usual rants of derision from each boxer and Eubank even bet £1,000 that he would floor Benn in the first round. But what happened on 18 November 1990 has since been hailed as one of the greatest fights ever to take place in the UK.

Nigel "The Dark Destroyer" Benn was born on 22 January 1964 in Ilford and is not the only member of his family to find sporting fame. His cousin is former England footballer Paul Ince. Benn began his professional career with a second-round knockout of Graeme Ahmed in January 1987 and won his first 22 bouts without having to go the distance. He suffered his first defeat in May 1989 against Michael Watson before claiming the WBO Middleweight title against Doug DeWitt less than a year later. He successfully defended his crown with a first-round victory over the much-feared Iran Barkley to set up this clash with Eubank.

Nicknamed "Simply the Best", Chris Eubank was born in Dulwich on 8 August 1966 and turned professional in 1985, registering a fourth-round victory over Tim Brown. Unusually for a British boxer, Eubank's first five fights were in the United States and he went on to win 40 out of his first 42 fights (he contested two draws, against Ray Close and Nigel Benn in 1993). He eventually lost his undefeated record to Steve Collins in March 1995.

Eubank entered the ring with his trademark vault over the ropes and both men stood composed as referee Richard Steele went through the preliminaries. The opening round saw Eubank land some telling punches while avoiding the champion's efforts as they both sounded each other out. The second round opened with a bang as Benn caught Eubank with several big right hands before the challenger countered with a superb left hook that rocked the Dark Destroyer and finished with a flurry of combination shots.

The third round again saw Eubank caught by a good right but many critics wondered why Benn was concentrating on more difficult head shots rather than pummelling his opponent's

body as he often did in fights. Maybe he was caught up in the emotion of the moment and was looking for the decisive shot that would tame Eubank once and for all. As it was, Eubank dodged Benn's biggest hits and counter-attacked with hooks and uppercuts of his own. Benn did aim for the body in the next round, but some big right hands from the challenger caused his right eye to swell. Eubank sensed he had the upper hand and began to dictate the pace of the fight but Benn battled back towards the bell.

Eubank confirmed his domination of the bout in round six by preventing Benn from employing the attacking style he normally preferred. Both boxers persevered with their jabs but it was the challenger who seemed to be winning the scoring. The seventh round saw Benn hit his opponent with a salvo of body blows but Eubank retaliated with his jab before launching a stinging left-right combination that inspired the champion to instigate a counter-attack of his own.

The next round was simply enthralling as Eubank continued jabbing while also throwing some telling punches, but Benn – having trouble seeing with one eye almost completely closed – responded with a thundering shot that floored the challenger. The ninth round saw Eubank launch another barrage at his opponent and suddenly Benn's legs went wobbly. Sensing his moment, Eubank rushed in to finish him off but – after giving Benn one more chance – the referee stopped the fight.

Both men displayed a grudging respect for each other after the fight, with Eubank claiming "he hit me with shots that I never knew existed" and observing that Benn had split his tongue during the bout.

The rematch was staged in October 1993, entitled "Judgement Day", and turned out to be a fascinating spectacle once more in front of 42,000 at Manchester's Old Trafford stadium. Eubank put his WBO Super Middleweight title on the line while Benn offered his WBC belt. After 12 gruelling rounds, the judges were unable to separate them and – with the scores tied at 113-115, 114-114, 115-113 – each kept his own crown.

By this time, Eubank was two years on from his defence against Michael Watson that left the challenger in a coma for 40 days and having to undergo six operations on his battered brain; Watson never fully recovered from this ordeal and remained partially paralysed. Benn would soon be facing a similar experience when he faced Gerald McClellan in 1995. After that 10th-round stoppage, Benn's opponent lost consciousness in the ring and emerged from hospital severely disabled.

RIDDICK BOWE v EVANDER HOLYFIELD
1992

Having been labelled a boxer with no heart at the 1988 Olympics in Seoul when he lost to Lennox Lewis in the Super Heavyweight final, Riddick Bowe finally laid that criticism to rest after 12 gruelling rounds in *Ring* magazine's Fight of the Year to claim the WBA, WBC and IBF Heavyweight crowns.

Evander "The Real Deal" Holyfield was born in Alabama on 19 October 1962 and had been the undisputed Cruiserweight champion before stepping up to Heavyweight. He had triumphed over James "Buster" Douglas, conqueror of Mike Tyson in 1990, and defended his crowns against such legendary fighters as George Foreman and Larry Holmes en route to this clash with Riddick Bowe.

Bowe, nicknamed "Big Daddy", was born on 10 August 1967 in New York and had his first professional fight in March 1989, a second-round victory over Lionel Butler. He soon grew in popularity and quickly gained a large following.

Both boxers were undefeated coming into this contest. Holyfield had won all his 28 fights (with 22 coming by way of a knockout) while Bowe boasted an impressive 27 knockouts from his 31 victories. Bowe at 6' 5" and with an 81" reach, however, enjoyed a physical advantage over his opponent who was a mere 6' 2" (78" reach). The challenger was also 30lbs heavier than the champion.

The fight started slowly but became more aggressive and volatile from the second round onwards. The champion found himself embroiled in a toe-to-toe brawl with Bowe, who unleashed a variety of punches including jabs, body shots, right uppercuts and a smashing left hook. The early rounds were very much Bowe's and it wasn't until the fifth round that Holyfield began to reassert himself with several left hooks. Although these were well-landed punches, they didn't seem to perturb the challenger at all.

Holyfield started the sixth round content to jab away at his opponent and keep his guard up but Bowe consistently found a way through. His combinations and uppercuts seemed laser-

guided and by the following round Holyfield discovered his right eye was beginning to close. The next few rounds continued in this fashion until the memorable 10th. Bowe caught his opponent with a tremendous left hook and a few well-timed combinations that rocked the champion. He staggered but managed to stay on his feet to deliver a counter-attack of his own.

Holyfield came out strongly in the 11th but Bowe's combinations and body shots were finally causing the damage he so desperately sought and he clobbered Holyfield with a left hook followed by a right to his head. The champion hit the canvas but recovered after a mandatory eight count and launched his own salvo at Bowe. Holyfield spent the remainder of the fight keeping his opponent away from him while trying to land some point-scoring punches of his own but it was too late.

When it was time for referee Joe Cortez to hold the winner's arm up, he lifted that of Riddick Bowe whose exploits had persuaded the judges to score the fight 115-112, 117-110, 117-110 in his favour. Bowe was very philosophical about the contest, saying: "I told you when this fight was over a lot of questions would be answered."

Even Holyfield's trainer George Benton had nothing but respect for the victor, claiming "I thought Bowe fought a tremendous fight. I thought he'd sag in the ninth or 10th round, but he didn't. He had the determination and he won one of the best fights I've ever seen in my life."

Bowe went on to score a first-round knockout over Michael Dokes and stopped Jesse Simpson in the second round before losing a points decision in the rematch to Holyfield (113-115, 114-115, 114-114). He added the WBO heavyweight title to his resumé in March 1995 with a sixth-round victory over Herbie Hide and successfully defended that crown against Jorge Luis Gonzalez three months later. A third fight with Holyfield took place in November 1995 with Bowe emerging victorious in the eighth round.

Holyfield lost the titles he had won from Bowe in 1993 to Michael Moorer a year later but reclaimed the WBA crown with a victory over Mike Tyson in 1996. He gained revenge on Moorer the following year, adding the IBF belt, before taking on WBC titleholder Lennox Lewis. Their first fight was judged a draw and the winner of the rematch would claim the WBA, WBC, IBF and the vacant IBO Heavyweight crowns. Lewis won a unanimous decision before Holyfield became a four-time winner of the WBA Heavyweight title with a unanimous decision victory over John Ruiz in August 2000. His next three title fights ended without a win, losing and then drawing the rematches with Ruiz before being on the wrong end of a points decision against Chris Bird for the vacant IBF Heavyweight crown.

GEORGE FOREMAN v MICHAEL MOORER 1994

There can't be many athletes in any sport who can claim to have regained the championship of the world after an interval of 20 years but that's exactly what 45-year-old George Foreman achieved on 5 November 1994 when he became the oldest boxer to ever win the Heavyweight title. Foreman had last held the title on 30 October 1974, when he took on Muhammad Ali in the infamous Rumble in the Jungle (see page 18) and had retired three years later to become a preacher.

George Foreman was born on 10 January 1949 in Texas and found himself in trouble with the authorities several times during his youth. He qualified for the US Olympic boxing team and won the Heavyweight gold at the 1968 Games in Mexico City. Foreman turned professional the following year and won his debut fight with a three-round knockout of Don Waldheim before going on to claim his first world title by knocking out champion Joe Frazier in January 1973.

His first venture back into the ring after a 10-year absence saw him stop Steve Zouski in the fourth round of their March 1987 bout and four years later he had a first shot at the title. He fought Evander Holyfield for the WBA, WBC and IBF Heavyweight belts but lost a unanimous decision (111-116, 110-117, 112-115) in April 1991 and three years later was again on the wrong end of a points decision (110-117, 110-117, 109-118) in his battle with Tommy Morrison for the vacant WBO title.

Michael Moorer – born on 12 November 1967 in New York – turned professional in March 1988 and had won the vacant WBO Light Heavyweight title nine months later. He stepped up to Heavyweight and claimed the vacant WBO in 1992 before winning a majority decision (115-114, 116-112, 114-114) over Evander Holyfield for the WBA and IBF belts two years later.

Foreman, at 17st 12lbs (6' 3" tall with an 82" reach), came into the bout two stone heavier than his opponent (6' 2" with a 78" reach) and incredibly he was 19 years older than

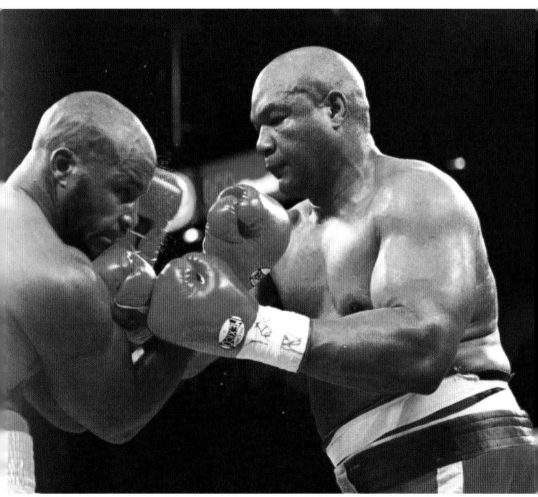

Moorer. His record, though, clearly demonstrated his vast experience with 72 victories (67 by way of knockout) and four defeats while Moorer boasted an undefeated 34-fight (30 knockouts) resumé.

The bout was staged at the MGM Grand Hotel in Las Vegas and Foreman – his physique showing the passage of time – was wearing the same shorts he had worn when he fought Ali all those years ago. The challenger entered the ring to the sounds of "If I Had A Hammer" while his opponent arrived accompanied by rap music and was holding the WBA and IBF Heavyweight belts above his head.

The champion started well, quickly thundering a left hook onto Foreman's head and followed this up with some decent jabs. Foreman stood and took all the punishment – as he would do all through the fight – waiting for the right moment to attack once Moorer had tired himself out. Once the round had finished, Foreman stood in his corner rather than sitting on the stool to be attended by his staff, engaging in a psychological battle with his opponent.

It was Moorer who landed the more accurate punches as the fight progressed and was well ahead on the judges' scorecards by the time of the 10th round. But, although he had hit the challenger with almost every weapon in his arsenal, Foreman was seemingly untroubled and about to rewrite the history books.

The historical moment began with a jackhammer right that rocked the champion. This was followed by a short left and a big right that put Moorer flat on his back on the canvas, with the champion unable to regain his feet before referee Joe Cortez counted him out. Foreman dropped to his knees and began praying for his opponent, but was soon told that Moorer was not badly injured.

Foreman was stripped of the WBA belt for refusing to fight Tony Tucker but went on to defend his IBF belt and claim the vacant WBU title with a majority decision (115-113, 115-113, 114-114) over Axel Schulz. The IBF stripped him of his title for not giving Schulz a rematch and he defended his WBU crown and added the IBA Heavyweight belt with a unanimous decision (119-109, 118-112, 117-111) in a non-sanctioned fight with Crawford Grimsley. One more victory followed, against Lou Savarese, before Foreman's final bout saw him defeated on points (113-117, 112-116, 114-114) by Shannon Briggs in 1997.

Foreman was scheduled to return to the ring two years later to fight Larry Holmes but these plans fell through and a suggested 2004 comeback was stopped by his wife. Instead, George Foreman can relive his memories and enjoy the earnings his Lean Mean Grilling Machine phenomenon has brought him. Moorer later reclaimed the IBF belt with a 1996 victory over Axel Schulz but lost his rematch with Holyfield the following year.

FRANK BRUNO v OLIVER McCALL
1995

Frank Bruno had established himself as the most popular fighter in Britain and earned himself a perennial place in the public's affection. He had also developed a unique rapport with commentator Harry Carpenter with the catchphrase "Know what I mean, 'Arry?" so his triumph over Oliver McCall – in his fourth shot at the title – in September 1995 was met with universal joy and admiration.

Frank Bruno was born in London on 16 November 1961 and was not even 10 years old when his mother introduced him to boxing at the Wandsworth Boys' Club. 10 years later, he became the youngest ever British Amateur Heavyweight champion but had to undergo surgery the following year to repair a damaged retina. He turned professional in 1982 and won his first fight, a first-round knockout of Lupe Guerra. In October 1985, he claimed the European Heavyweight title with a fourth-round stoppage of Anders Eklund and got his first title chance the following year.

Tim Witherspoon was his opponent but the fight was stopped in the 11th round. He got his second chance in February 1989 but was up against the undefeated Mike Tyson who was at the height of his career. Having hit the canvas in the first round, Bruno battled on but was stopped in the fifth. Undaunted, Bruno re-established himself as a contender and was rewarded with a title clash with Lennox Lewis four years later but this bout was stopped in the seventh round and Bruno found himself still awaiting a world title.

Oliver McCall was born in Chicago on 21 April 1965 and twice won the city's amateur Golden Gloves title. His first professional fight was a first-round knockout of Lou Bailey in November 1985 but he suffered the first defeat of his career in the following fight against Joey Christjohn. He won his WBC Heavyweight belt with a controversial second-round knockout of Lennox Lewis. Referee Lupe Garcia stopped the fight after a big right had put the champion on the deck but Lewis later insisted he had been perfectly *compus mentis* and that the contest should have been allowed to continue. McCall successfully defended his title against Larry Holmes to set up this clash with Bruno.

McCall had earlier escaped a fine from the World Boxing Council for claiming that he wanted to inflict serious damage on his opponent but it was the champion who had to protect his left eye from closing completely for the majority of the fight. True, Bruno did land some big rights, but he was never the fastest or most nimble boxer and McCall didn't seem to be troubled too much. In the final round – perhaps sensing that he was behind in the judges' scoring – McCall unleashed a barrage of punches that had Bruno holding on for the final bell.

It was only the second time that Bruno had ever been the distance, and he registered a unanimous decision over McCall with the judges scoring the fight 117-111, 117-111, 115-113 in his favour. Bruno had finally achieved what he had set out to do all those years ago and was a world champion. It was the greatest moment in his career and he even bought the ring in which the fight was fought.

He attempted to defend his WBC Heavyweight title against Mike Tyson the following year but suffered a similar fate as he had previously. The American claimed the title with a third-round stoppage and this proved to be Bruno's final fight as he suffered a detached retina. Bruno was advised by medical experts that any further bouts might bring about a permanent loss of sight. He did apply to the British Boxing Board of Control for his licence in 2003, claiming that he wanted to fight Olympic champion Audley Harrison but this comeback never materialised.

But it is perhaps outside the ring that Frank Bruno gained most of his popularity. He established a successful career in entertainment, starring in numerous pantomimes and being a regular chat-show guest and after-dinner speaker. But some of his antics became increasingly bizarre – including claims that he slept in the boxing ring in his garden – and culminated in him being sectioned under the Mental Health Act in September 2003 and diagnosed with depression. He had earlier announced that he would stand as a Conservative MP in 2001 with the slogan "Don't be a plank, vote for Frank!" and was devastated by the news in April 2002 that his former trainer George Francis had been found hanged in his London home.

McCall had a rematch with Lennox Lewis in February 1997 for the vacant WBC Heavyweight title but the Londoner exacted revenge for his defeat three years earlier and claimed the crown with a fifth-round stoppage. Undeterred, McCall continued boxing and eventually claimed the vacant WBC Fecarbox Heavyweight title with a fourth-round victory over Darroll Wilson in September 2006.

STEVE COLLINS v CHRIS EUBANK 1995

It was in perhaps bizarre circumstances that the undefeated WBO Super Middleweight titleholder Chris Eubank took on challenger Steve Collins in March 1995. Eubank had been lined up to meet Ray Close in a rematch of their drawn 1993 fight but the Irishman had failed a brain scan so Collins took his place. He immediately began taunting the champion and claiming that he was undergoing hypnosis in order to win the fight.

Eubank retaliated with a quote that was misunderstood in the press and which only added to the public's dislike of the brash champion. He had stated that he could potentially kill his opponent but what he meant was that it was dangerous for a boxer to enter the ring in a hypnotised state because his brain would not necessarily accept defeat. This might lead to more serious injuries than would have otherwise been incurred.

Chris Eubank (born on 8 August 1966 in Brighton) began his professional career with a points victory over Tim Brown in October 1985. He went on to establish himself as a fighter to be respected and won the WBC International Middleweight title from Hugo Antonio Corti in March 1990. By the end of that year, he had taken Nigel Benn's WBO Middleweight title (see page 54) and went on to defend it three times against Dan Sherry, Gary Stretch and Michael Watson.

He fought Watson again for the vacant WBO Super Middleweight title in an ill-fated bout that changed the Londoner's life forever after he was left with permanent brain damage. Eubank went on to record 14 successful defences of this title until he met Collins.

Steve Collins (aka the "Celtic Warrior") was born in Dublin on 21 July 1964 and was a strong, confident and experienced boxer who had turned professional in 1986. He had already claimed the WBO Middleweight belt in May 1994 but was keen to add Eubank's scalp to his list of victims.

At the end of the day, Eubank should have concentrated on his own tactics and need not have concerned himself with the hypnotism story because it was later alleged that this was just a ruse to unsettle the champion. It obviously worked because Eubank lost his undefeated record and suffered only the fourth knockdown of his career.

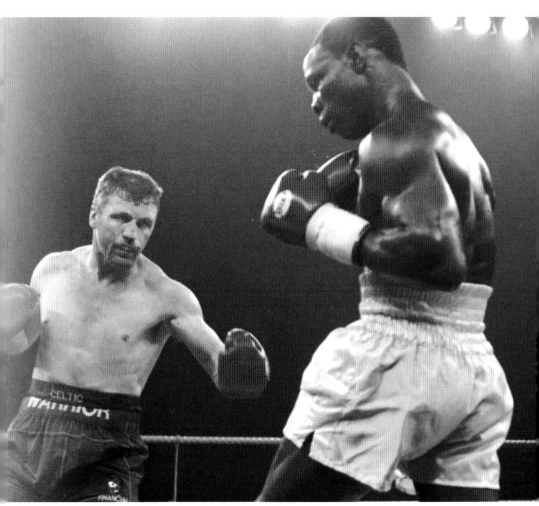

STEVE COLLINS v CHRIS EUBANK

Having been hyped to the limit, the contest in the Republic of Ireland was an eagerly-anticipated bout and neither the crowd nor the millions watching on television were disappointed. The fight turned out to be an exciting battle between the two boxers with Eubank being knocked down in the eighth round. He recovered to put Collins on the canvas in the 10th round but found himself losing his title in his 15th defence when referee Ron Lipton announced the judges' unanimous decision (113-117, 112-114, 112-114).

The rematch in Cork six months later was another grudge match and Eubank really had the bit between his teeth. He had recorded first-round victories over Bruno Ruben Godoy and Jose Ignacio Barruetabena between the two Collins fights and was confident of reclaiming his title. Collins, on the other hand, hadn't fought since the first match but had the advantage of fighting in the country of his birth.

Collins started the fight like a man possessed and constantly attacked the challenger. Eubank seemed happy to take the punishment and pick his punches carefully. He may have landed the better punches but it was the sheer quantity of blows struck by the Celtic Warrior that persuaded the judges to score him the winner in a split decision (115-113, 115-113, 114-115).

Having been able to call himself a world champion for five years, Eubank was devastated at being unable to regain his title but set about re-establishing himself as a contender. He demolished Luis Dionisio Barrera in five rounds and Camilo Alarcon in four to set up a 1997 clash with Joe Calzaghe for the vacant WBO Super Middleweight title. No longer "Simply the Best", Eubank found himself on the canvas in the first round and despite recovering to go the distance was on the wrong end of a unanimous decision (111-116, 110-118, 109-118).

He stepped up to contest the WBO Cruiserweight title with Carl Thompson the following year but lost on the judges' scorecards (113-114, 113-114, 113-116) even though he had the champion on the deck in the fourth round. The rematch in July 1998 proved to be Eubank's last professional bout. The fight was stopped on medical grounds after the ninth round with the challenger's left eye completely closed and his final record read 45 victories (23 knockouts), five defeats and two draws.

Collins went on to successfully defend his title six times against Cornelius Carr, Neville Brown, Nigel Benn (twice), Frederic Seillier and Craig Cummings before retiring as champion in 1997. It was rumoured that he was going to make a comeback against Roy Jones Jr in 1999 but this never materialised.

"PRINCE" NASEEM HAMED v KEVIN KELLEY
1997

The undisputed showman of the ring put paid to Kevin Kelley's challenge in four rounds on 19 December 1997 in his first fight at New York's Madison Square Garden. "Prince" Naseem Hamed's entrance took almost as much time as the fight lasted, but the clash was voted *Ring* magazine's Fight of the Year and was one of the champion's toughest ever defences.

As befitting his self-bestowed status as the best fighter in the world, he arrived at New York on a British Airways Concorde but this bout would prove to be anything but a breeze. It was the first time in his career that Hamed – who had angered critics and fans alike in the past with his arrogant style that included mocking his opponents – had to abandon his glove-by-his-side approach and actually work on defending himself although he had temporarily adopted this tactic in his 1996 two-round meeting with Daniel Alicea. The discussion still continues to this day as to the reason for this struggle, with most arguing that he was fighting a better calibre of opponent.

Naseem Hamed (born on 12 February 1974) was born to Yemeni parents who emigrated to Sheffield and he began boxing at the age of seven in order to help him develop some self-defence. He won his first (WBO) Featherweight title in 1995 with an eighth-round knockout of defending champion Steve Robinson. Hamed, at 5' 4" and 126lbs, came into the fight with an impressive unbeaten record of 29-0 with 27 knockouts.

Kevin "Flushing Flash" Kelley was born on 29 June 1967 and his first professional fight was against Willie Barnes in September 1988, a bout that ended with a second-round knockout. He enjoyed both a height (at 5' 7") and reach advantage (71" to Hamed's 64") but entered the ring at the same weight. He brought with him a more experienced 47-2-2 (32 knockouts) record but had rarely been up against anyone of Hamed's ability.

The spectacle began with both southpaw boxers missing with their initial right hooks and it was Hamed who seemed to settle first, landing a few decent jabs on the American. But it was the Flushing Flash who scored the first big punch of the evening. With Hamed leaning back, Kelly caught him with a jab that just spurred on the Englishman. He launched one of his trademark

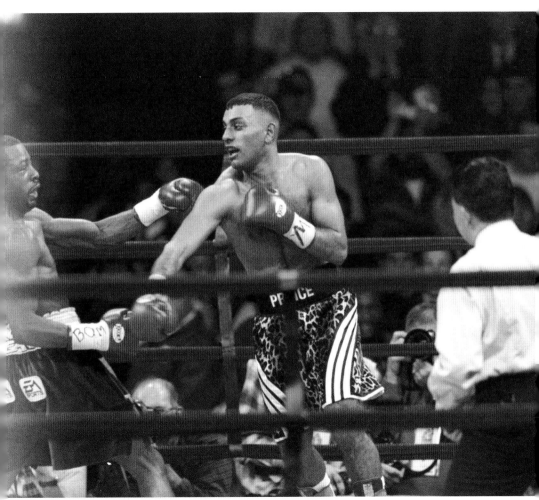

leaping punches into Kelley's face before following this up with a speedy succession of jabs. As the round drew to a close, Hamed changed tactics and adopted a more orthodox defending stance but Kelley landed a right on the champion's chin that sent him crashing to the canvas. He was up by the count of two, but both his opponent and the home crowd were wildly encouraged by this display of vulnerability.

The second round saw Hamed and Kelley exchanging jabs with the American coming out of the exchange with the upper hand. His jabs had pushed Hamed onto the ropes and, after the younger man had missed with a swinging punch, Kelley scored one on his chin that forced him to stumble. Another fierce right to the head and referee Benjy Esteves Jr had no option but to give a mandatory eight count after both his gloves had touched the floor. Hamed was out for revenge and clocked Kelley after his momentum had carried him into the ropes but the referee declared no knockdown. But it wasn't long before the champion had the challenger legitimately on the deck. A solid right caught Kelley but he was up at the count of four before attempting to lay a wild barrage on Hamed. The round ended with Hamed showing the side of his persona that most disliked as he taunted his opponent but it was Kelley who was beginning to show signs of trauma around his eyes.

The third round saw Hamed come out on top after some accurate jabs and right hands nailed their target but it was the fourth round that would provide the fireworks. After a jabbing duel, Hamed caught Kelley with a couple of short lefts on the chin and the American was down for the second time in the fight. Although he was up by the time the referee had reached six, he was obviously dazed and in the final minute of the round Hamed connected with a superb left hook. Landing on his back with his eyes closed, Kelley struggled to get upright before the count finished but, seeing his precarious state, the referee stopped the contest.

Hamed went on to fight another six successful title defences before being dethroned by Marco Antonio Barrera in 2001 while Kelley lost his next world title fight against Erik Morales in 2000 but he did win a majority decision (116-112, 115-113, 114-114) over Humberto Soto for the vacant NABA Super Featherweight Title two years later.

"PRINCE" NASEEM HAMED v KEVIN KELLEY   77

LENNOX LEWIS v MIKE TYSON
2002

After all the hype and bravado, this fight turned out to be more of a one-sided battle than many thought possible. When the fight was announced in January 2002, "Iron" Mike Tyson and Lennox "The Lion" Lewis had to be pulled apart. Indeed, Tyson was forced to pay his opponent $335,000 out of his fight purse for biting him at the press conference.

The organisers were not taking any chances on hostilities, which began earlier than scheduled, when the fight did eventually take place on 8 June, with a dozen or so security guards in the ring with orders to keep the boxers apart until the first bell. Several states – as well as the boxing mecca of Las Vegas – had refused Tyson a licence in view of his sordid history but Memphis bid $12 million to win the right to stage the fight that was eventually held at the Pyramid.

Lewis – born on 2 September 1965 and holder of the WBC, IBF and IBO Heavyweight titles – went into the fight with a 40-2-1 record (31 knockouts) while Tyson's read 49-4, 2 no contests (43 knockouts) but he had the physical advantage at 6' 5" tall, an 84" reach and weighing 246¼lbs. Bear in mind that Tyson (30 June 1966) stood at only 5' 10", had a 71" reach and weighed in at 234lbs.

The opening round proved to be a cagey affair with both fighters feeling their way and sounding out their opponent. Tyson came out quickest and landed a couple of decent jabs while Lewis made his power felt with a couple of uppercuts.

The second round was Lewis's all the way from the bell. After being cautioned by referee Eddie Cotton for holding and hitting, Lewis landed a beautiful right uppercut and began concentrating on his jab. After being hit by a second uppercut, Tyson – realising that he was having difficulty getting to the champion – began lunging in the vain hope that one of his punches would land somewhere near the mark. This strategy didn't work, however, as Lewis continued landing telling punches. By the end of the round, Lewis was in complete control and a dazed Tyson wasn't sure what to do next.

Although Tyson did come out with a purpose in the third round, it was Lewis who again controlled proceedings with another right hand to the jaw and several accurate jabs. Tyson did

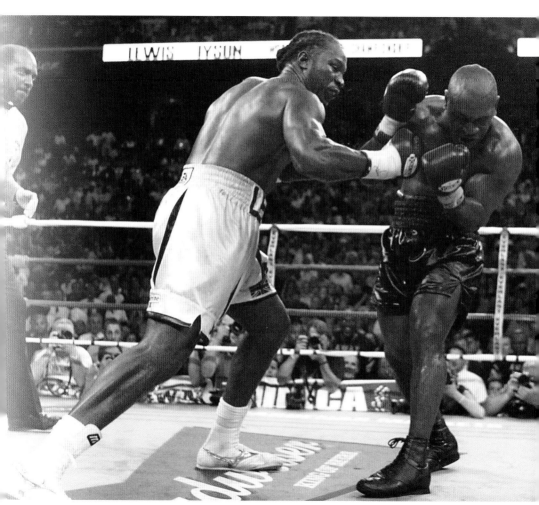

manage to land a couple of weak punches but soon found he had been cut over the right eye. This spurred him on and he landed a left hook on Lewis's head before the champion scored well with a combination.

The fourth round saw a continuation of the one-sided affair, with Lewis consistently getting through with his punches while Tyson seemed to be unable to stop or evade them. A fierce right from Lewis saw the cut over Tyson's eye worsen but more alarming was the sight of "Iron" Mike walking into punches he used to dodge with ease. Several more vicious punches followed before Lewis was docked a point for pushing Tyson to the canvas.

His corner worked hard between rounds to patch up his right eye, but was left with twice as much work after the fifth round. Lewis inflicted even more damage on his face with several pinpoint jabs and rights that split the skin over Tyson's left eye. The demolition was almost complete and small pools of blood were beginning to spatter the canvas.

Now having difficulty seeing, Tyson suffered even more punishment in the sixth round. Lewis, with the outcome of the bout firmly in his own hands, took the fight to the American and systematically concentrated on making his shots count. He landed fierce rights, lefts and uppercuts that left Tyson trudging to his corner at the sound of the bell.

While Tyson came out at the start of the seventh, it wasn't long before normal service was resumed and he again found himself on the receiving end of Lewis's battering rams. A series of jabs and punches left Tyson's nose bleeding in sympathy with his eyes and it was clear that the fight was not going to last much longer.

In fact, it didn't even last one more round as a calculating Lewis bade his time while landing accurate punches. A trio of uppercuts saw Tyson's knees give way but he didn't actually go down. The referee gave him a mandatory eight count nonetheless and Lewis followed this up with another crashing right hand to the jaw which this time did send the American to the canvas. With blood pouring down his face, Tyson clutched his glove to his right eye and was counted out.

Lewis, who relinquished his IBF title, went on to successfully defend against Vitali Klitschko the following year when the fight was stopped due to a cut suffered by the Ukrainian before retiring. Tyson, however, found his indestructible tag was a thing of the past and – although he beat Clifford Etienne – lost twice in succession to Danny Williams and Kevin McBride.

ROY JONES JR v JOHN RUIZ
2003

When Roy Jones Jr thrashed John Ruiz on 1 March 2003, he became the first Middleweight champion to successfully move up to win the Heavyweight crown since "Ruby" Bob Fitzsimmons in 1897.

Roy Levesta Jones Jr was born on 16 January 1969 in Florida and won the Junior Middleweight silver medal at the 1988 Seoul Olympics. He turned professional in May 1989 with a second-round victory over Ricky Randall. Considered by many to be the best pound for pound fighter in the world, the Boxing Writers' Association of America declared Jones the Fighter of the Decade in 1999.

John "The Quiet Man" Ruiz was born in Puerto Rico on 4 January 1972 and his professional debut was a unanimous decision over Kevin Parker in August 1992. He had won the WBA Heavyweight belt in a rematch with Evander Holyfield in March 2001 that had ended in a unanimous decision (116-110, 115-111, 114-111).

Jones came into the fight at 5' 11" and 13st 11lbs while the 6' 2" Ruiz weighed in at 16st 9lbs. Both orthodox fighters, Ruiz (whose record stood at 38-4-1, 27 KOs) also enjoyed a 4" reach advantage over Jones (47-1, 38 KOs).

The first round started with Ruiz on the offensive, pushing Jones back onto the ropes, but referee Jay Nady was soon warning the champion about low blows. After weathering the initial onslaught, Jones began to find his rhythm and started to land some telling punches while Ruiz pulled him in close when his blows became too accurate. The round ended with both fighters having landed big right hands and the stage was set for a fascinating encounter.

The second round saw the champion come out wary of Jones's big punches and he began to flinch when he thought one was coming his way. Half way through the round, Ruiz walked straight into one of Jones's sledgehammer left hooks and was later the recipient of another quick salvo. The challenger took a step to his left and landed another crunching right uppercut to Ruiz's face as the champion stood in the centre of the ring.

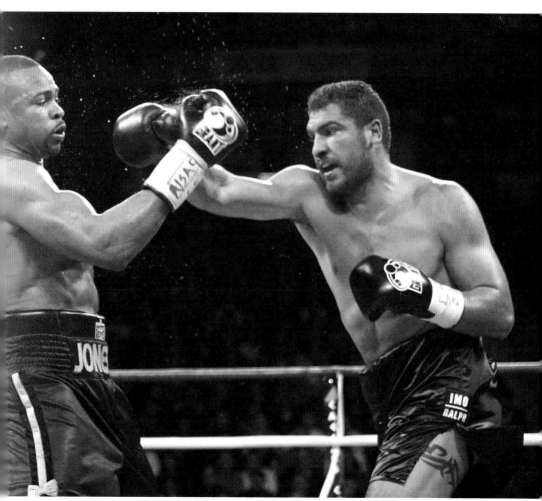

ROY JONES JR v JOHN RUIZ   83

The smaller, more mobile fighter was using his agility to outbox and evade his opponent's punches and it was working. The third round saw Jones land series after series of jabs to Ruiz's face and body before a brilliant left hook smashed into his ribs. He obviously felt that punch as he kept his elbows close to his sides after that but was unable to stop another big right to his face just before the bell.

Jones drew first blood in the fourth round when he landed a stinging right cross to Ruiz's face that made his eyes water and nose bleed. The champion was unable to prevent Jones from dancing and ducking, throwing punches from whichever angle he pleased and it was obvious that this was turning into a one-sided bout. In the final half of the round, Jones connected with two left hooks and a left-right combination that only aggravated Ruiz's condition and the champion slowly retreated to his corner for a brief respite.

And so the tale of destruction went on. Jones landed further telling punches in the sixth having goaded his opponent into action by standing with his arms at his sides. A left hook to the jaw was swiftly followed by a right to his nose before a three-punch salvo to the head saw Ruiz clinging onto Jones and the ropes. The champion did manage to get his opponent onto the ropes at the start of the eighth and land a few powerhouse shots of his own but Jones escaped to the centre of the ring and continued to pick off the bigger man. Two left hooks got through Ruiz's defences before an almighty right hand landed smack in the middle of his face, smearing him with blood.

The ninth round saw Jones ease off though Ruiz was unable to get back into the fight but the battering resumed in the 10th and 11th. Jones caught the champion with several three-punch combinations to the head and all he had to do in the final round was avoid a lucky knockout blow from his opponent. He preferred to dodge the few cumbersome punches that Ruiz threw and emerged triumphant at the final bell.

The fight was scored as follows: Jerry Roth 116-112; Stanley Christodoulou 118-110; and Duane Ford 117-111. Ruiz blamed the referee for the loss, claiming that he "did not let me fight my fight".

This was Jones' only Heavyweight bout as he relinquished the belt and moved back to Light Heavyweight the following November to secure a majority decision over Antonio Tarver before losing in the second round of the rematch in May 2004. Ruiz defended his title four times before losing a majority decision (114-116, 114-114, 113-116) to Nicolay Valuev in December 2005.

JOE CALZAGHE v JEFF LACY
2006

Having held the WBO Super Middleweight world title since he outpointed Chris Eubank for the vacant crown in Sheffield in October 1997, Joe Calzaghe had been desperate to unify the belts but found the opportunity hard to come by. It was originally planned to unify the WBO and IBF titles in November 2005 but the fight had to be rescheduled due to a break sustained to the metacarpal in his left hand.

The match did eventually take place on 5 March 2006 and it proved well worth the wait. At the MEN Arena in Manchester, "The Italian Dragon" – with 40 wins, 31 by knockout – faced up to "Left Hook" Lacy and many critics forecast that the American would overwhelm Calzaghe with his constant pressure and hard punches. Even Lacy himself predicted that there would be no 12th-round bell.

Calzaghe was born to a Welsh mother and a Sardinian father in Hammersmith, London (on 23 March 1972), but moved to Wales at a very early age. He started boxing when he was just nine years old and quickly earned the nicknames "The Pride of Wales" and "The Italian Dragon" with his first professional fight being against Paul Hanlon at Cardiff Arms Park. He won this bout – on the under card of Frank Bruno's title clash with Lennox Lewis – by a technical knockout in round one.

Jeff Lacy, born on 12 May 1977 in Florida, made his professional debut in February 2001 with a first-round knockout of Jerald Lowe and contested his first world title in October 2004. He faced Syd "The Jewel" Vanderpool for the vacant IBF Super Middleweight title and stopped the Canadian in the eighth round before adding the IBO Super Middleweight belt to his resumé with an eight-round victory over Robin Reid in August 2005. His style has been compared by some critics to that of Mike Tyson, although they have also noted that he is slower and not as well co-ordinated.

At 6' tall with a 73" reach, the southpaw Calzaghe compared favourably with the orthodox Lacy (5' 10" and a 74" reach) and there was only a one-pound difference in their weights.

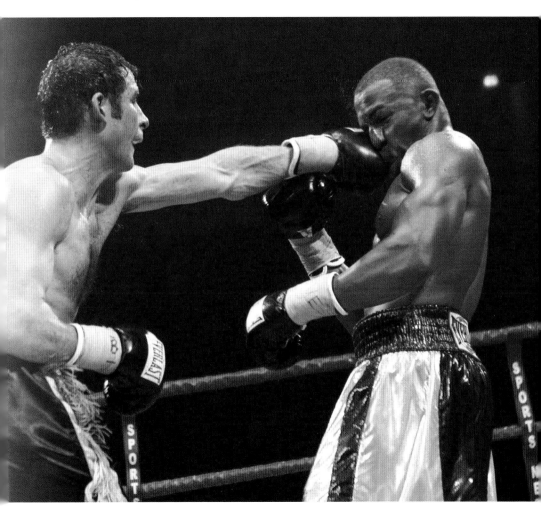

Although it was claimed that Lacy had faced some mismatched opponents in his previous 22 fights that had produced 21 victories, 17 by knockout (his June 2004 fight against Vitali Tsypko was declared a no contest after the Ukrainian suffered a cut to his head that had been caused by a head butt), he had beaten a creditable boxer in Reid. The "Grim Reaper" had never before been on the canvas, but Lacy decked him four times.

As the fight started, Calzaghe showed his mobility and punching ability from the outset with jabs and uppercuts finding their mark. Only a few of Lacy's punches hit the mark though, and the majority of them missed the target. The second round saw the Pride of Wales taking a firm grip on the contest with his combination punches already having made Lacy's nose bleed.

The fourth round saw Lacy take even more of a battering as the one-sided fight continued. Calzaghe threw a combination of left and rights which succeeded in cutting the American's left eye…both of his eyes were in a similar state by the end of the round and the doctor had a close look at his face before allowing him to continue.

It seemed as if Lacy had no answer to Calzaghe's onslaught but he did land one of his trademark left hooks in the seventh but found it enraged his opponent into a ferocious barrage of punches. Calzaghe caught him with a good left as the round ended but the American managed to stay on his feet and enjoyed his best round of the contest in the eighth.

With Calzaghe trying to find the knockout punch, he was leaving himself more open to counter-attacks than he should have and Lacy landed a big left in the ninth but the adopted Welshman just shrugged it off. Calzaghe was docked a point in the 11th round for punching round Lacy's back during a break but by that time it was irrelevant.

The final round saw another Calzaghe onslaught with a perfect right hand knocking Lacy onto the canvas for the first time. He survived the count and managed to cling on for the rest of the round but it was clear who had won by the bell. The three judges, Nelson Vázquez (105-119), Roy Francis (107-119) and Adalaide Byrd (107-119) scored the fight unanimously and overwhelmingly in Calzaghe's favour while Lacy found his perfect record tarnished.

Joe Calzaghe successfully defended his titles against Australian Sakio Bika (another unanimous decision after 12 rounds) in October 2006 and was named the BBC Wales Sports Personality of the Year two months later. He was also nominated for the BBC British Sports Personality of the Year won by Princess Anne's daughter Zara Phillips.

RICKY HATTON v LUIS COLLAZO 2006

Named *Ring Magazine's* Fighter of the Year in December 2005, Ricky "The Hitman" Hatton (born on 6 October 1978) had just overcome Carlos Maussa with a knockout in the ninth round to unify the WBA and IBF Light Welterweight titles. However, he relinquished his IBF belt after he refused to fight the number one contender Naoufel Ben Rabah and moved up a weight to challenge for the WBA Welterweight crown.

On 13 May 2006, he took on Luis Collazo (born on 22 April 1981) at Boston's TD Bankworth Gardens. Collazo, a native New Yorker, had won 26 of his previous 27 fights – including 12 knockouts – and at 5' 9" and with a 72" reach had an advantage over Hatton (5' 7" with a 67" reach). Hatton came into the fight on the back of an unbeaten 40-match run that included 30 knockouts.

It was Hatton's first fight in the United States for eight years – since he had been on the under card of Prince Naseem Hamed v Wayne McCullough – but he handled the pressure like a seasoned veteran. A memorial 10-count was tolled in tribute to former world champion Floyd Patterson, who had died two days earlier.

The first round saw Hatton put the New Yorker on the canvas after just 12 seconds but Collazo recovered and, despite a barrage of uppercuts, right hands and left hooks, managed to stay on his feet for the rest of the round. The second round saw more of the same, with Hatton picking his shots and landing several left hooks to his opponent's body. Collazo tried to go on the offensive, but Hatton's attack was too accurate and ferocious. He did manage to land a right jab but the Stockport-born fighter caught Collazo off balance.

The third round saw Collazo find his feet and he realised his best chance of success was to try and disrupt Hatton's rhythm. This was an effective tactic and, although Hatton threw more punches than his opponent (who also suffered a cut on the top of the head after an accidental clash), Collazo's attacks were more accurate. The American

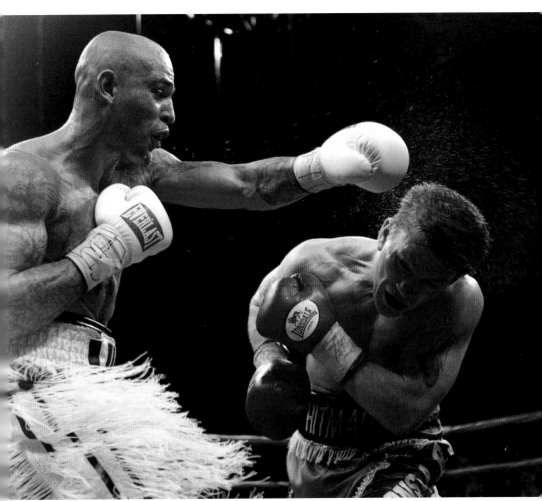

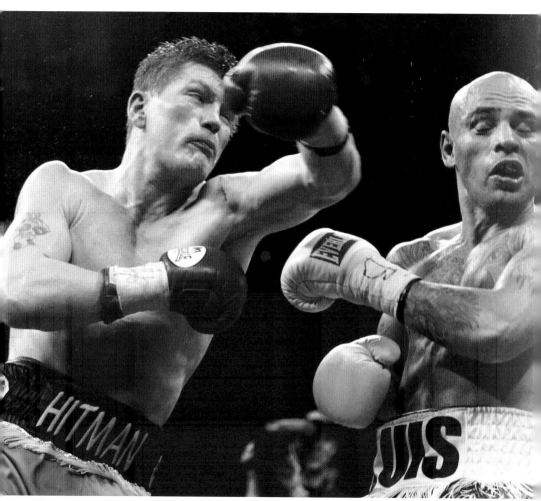

claimed the fourth round as well with some blistering right hooks but Hatton soaked it all up. The two men stood toe to toe and tried to batter each other into submission.

Collazo was growing in confidence as Hatton's workrate slowed in the sixth round as the Hitman was found wanting in reply to the younger man's speedy hands and feet. But he did manage to land some decent shots to his opponent's body. In the seventh, Hatton changed his tactics and came back into the fight. Now throwing right-hand punches from close range, he found more success as Collazo seemed to tire.

The eighth round saw Hatton seemingly revitalised as Collazo appeared to be finding the pace too much. The American scored heavily with a beautiful right that rocked his opponent's chin, but Hatton came back with a frantic barrage of heavy punches to claim the round. After the bell, Hatton continued his quick onslaught, trying to prevent Collazo from having the time to plan his next move. He landed some well-timed right jabs but was starting to show some wear and tear around his left eye.

The 10th round saw a much better contribution from Collazo as he dodged Hatton's ineffectual efforts yet landed some telling ones of his own. The American hit the canvas but this was declared a push and he ended the round with a right-left combination that again rocked the Englishman's head. Hatton claimed the 11th round despite repeatedly being clobbered by his opponent's southpaw right.

The 12th and final round saw the two men engage in the last chapter of an exciting battle. Collazo tried in vain to find the knockout punch and had Hatton on the deck but the referee decided not to take a count. Hatton continued to push forward but it was clearly the American's round.

There followed a tense and nervous wait for the judges' decision and when it arrived it proved to be unanimous. Two score cards gave the fight to Hatton by 115-112 while it was closer on the third at 114-113 and he was crowned the new WBA Welterweight champion of the world. Blows were reported as Hatton registered 259/741 (a success rate of 30%) while Collazo landed 213 out of 712 (also 30%).

Collazo, who many thought had done enough to retain his title, would be on the wrong end of another unanimous decision when he fought "Sugar" Shane Mosley in February 2007 for the WBC interim Welterweight crown. Hatton, on the other hand, recaptured the unified IBF and IBO Light Welterweight titles by beating Juan Urango to a unanimous verdict in Las Vegas on 20 January 2007.

ALSO AVAILABLE IN THIS SERIES

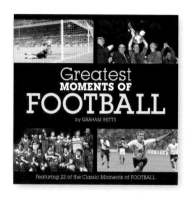

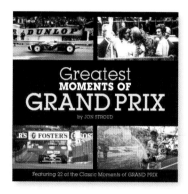

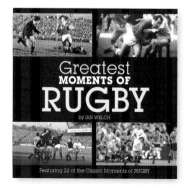

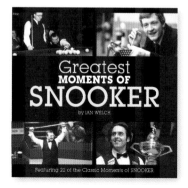

THE PICTURES IN THIS BOOK WERE PROVIDED COURTESY OF THE FOLLOWING.

GETTY IMAGES
101 Bayham Street, London NW1 0AG

PA PHOTOS
www.paphotos.com

Concept and Creative Direction:
VANESSA and KEVIN GARDNER

Design and Artwork: KEVIN GARDNER

Image research: ELLIE CHARLESTON

PUBLISHED BY GREEN UMBRELLA PUBLISHING

Publishers:
JULES GAMMOND and VANESSA GARDNER

Written by: IAN WELCH